Make your own
Greetings Cards

Projects written and created by
Margit Rigden

imagine THAT!™

Imagine That! is an imprint of Top That! Publishing plc
Tide Mill Way, Woodbridge, Suffolk, IP12 IAP
www.topthatpublishing.com

Contents

Introduction

Welcome to the world of card making – an inspiring selection of craft projects that allow you to make and personalise your own greetings cards for those special occasions. Making your own cards is not only easy, it's fun, too.

Packed into this book you will find both simple and challenging ways to create fabulous cards that will be a joy to make and receive. Learn the basic techniques in card making by following the easy step-by-step instructions and enjoy the full-colour photography of the finished pieces.

All of the following projects are designed so that by simply changing the colours or the materials you can adapt a card to suit any occasion or individual. Specific greetings have also been omitted, enabling you to choose your own message.

As you work through the ideas you're sure to realise that the creative possibilities in making your own greetings cards are endless, and there are often new craft products on the market that can make your work even more special.

This book, perfect for inspiring beginners, will also give the more advanced crafter some new ideas. Enjoy discovering how to create your own cards!

Basic Tools

Before you can start making your own greetings cards you'll need to gather together a few basic tools, most of which will probably already be lying around the house. This pack provides you with a selection of handy items that will be useful when completing these particular projects, but the list opposite includes other essentials and frequently used items you'll want to have close at hand.

You won't have all these tools but don't worry – making your own cards is about using your imagination and creativity, so don't be afraid to improvise and adapt the projects in this book.

As your skills improve you're bound to want to expand your collection of tools, and specialised materials can be found in craft shops or haberdashery departments. Read on to find out how to get the most out of your materials and learn some of the basic techniques that can be put to good use on all cards.

ESSENTIAL ITEM.

* Metal ruler
* Craft knife
* Cutting mat
* Soft pencil
* Good quality rubber
* Scissors – paper, precision and pattern-bladed craft scissors
* Glue – paper glue and stronger glue, such as silicone glue or PVA, glitter glue will also come in handy
* Sticky tape – single- and double-sided
* A selection of papers in different shapes, colours, prints etc for background
* Plain and coloured card, in sheets and folded
* Embossing tool
* Glitter in various colours
* Sticky foam pads
* Assortment of ribbons
* Fabric flowers and other embellishments
* Peel-off stickers (very fin stickers, in various design available from craft shops in borders, greetings etc
* A selection of basic punches such as stars, hearts, snowflakes etc

Materials

Colouring

You can use any medium to add colour to your work: watercolour paints, watercolour pencils, pastels, chalks, pencils, double-sided brush pens, even felt-tip pens if you require bright, primary colours.

Colouring pencils and brush pens from leading manufacturers are some of the easiest to use and offer a wide range of colours suitable for sensitive work.

Colouring pencils

Use branded quality colouring pencils to draw soft lines close to each other moving in up, down and across motions; smudging with a cotton bud afterwards will give a smooth, continuous colour. For darker shades use a contrasting colour, or go over with the same pencil, until you achieve the shade you want.

Brush pens

Start with the lightest colours and build up to the darker shades. Highlights should be created by leaving small areas of white; this will help give your work a three-dimensional feel.

Troubleshooting

White correction fluid can be used for accidentally coloured in spaces, highlights in eyes, or the centre of flowers, for example. Pencil smudges from your fingers can be rubbed out with a good-quality eraser. Mistakes made with brush pens can be covered up with a strategically placed sticker.

Card and paper stock

Try to use good quality card or paper, since the quality of your materials will reflect on your work. For inserts, however, you can use normal printing paper quality. Use a smooth, white ink jet paper for a more elegant finish. Be wary of recycled materials, as applied colours and paints can run.

Always ask at the shop where you are buying if the material you like is suitable for the purpose you want it for.

Be aware of paper weights – thin card starts at 120 gsm. Really thick will be anything over 230 gsm and is difficult to use in card making.

Glue and raised images

There are a number of different types of glue used in card making. Thin paper glue is needed to stick backing paper smoothly to base cards, and also to add fine glitter detail. However, silicone glue or thick, strong glue is needed to secure larger embellishments, or to give items such as leaves and flowers shape and depth.

Silicone glue takes time to dry, allowing plenty of opportunity for re-positioning, adjustments and moulding. However, to get the most out of your tube, remove a small blob with a cocktail stick, close the tube and then work with the glue on a piece of paper.

Alternatively, you can use sticky foam pads or 'spacers' to create a three-dimensional effect. These are double-sided and produce flat, straight layers.

Troubleshooting

To remove glue marks on your work, allow them to dry completely then gently rub off. Any attempts to remove the glue while it is still wet will result in further smudges and marks.

Ribbon

Ribbon of any size, shape or colour can be used in your card-making adventures. There are various ways you can use ribbon. Look closely at the projects featured later in this book, where ribbon has been used along the spines of cards, stuck on the front and even threaded through the card, to give beautiful results.

Scissors for paper craft

There are many different pattern-bladed scissors available and new cutting designs arrive regularly. You cannot cut hair or material with these scissors so they are quite safe for children to use, although younger children should always be supervised by an adult.

The deckle-edged pattern (see scissors bottom right) is the most common and easy to use, as you can move your scissors along the card or paper edge without having to worry about the continuity of the pattern. All other patterns need careful re-positioning to continue the sequences neatly.

To cut straight lines you can either draw a line to follow, keeping the inside blade line parallel with the card edge; or use the outside of your scissors as a guide along the card edge.

You can also make paper ribbons with the pattern-bladed scissors. To create a paper ribbon, cut along a straight edge of a long piece of paper. Turn your paper, then position your scissors a few millimetres parallel from the first cut. Line up the pattern and cut along the length of the paper keeping the width constant.

Examples of effects using pattern-bladed scissors

Cathedral

Scallop Tree

Pinking   Scallop

Envelopes

With all the detailed work that goes into your cards and the materials added to the front of your designs, it's wise to post your cards in a padded envelope. Alternatively, you can make your own envelopes from white or coloured paper. Simply open out a standard envelope, copy the shape and folds, adjusting the size to fit your own cards. Use paper glue to stick the envelope edges in position.

Recycling

Bought cards can easily be recycled and incorporated into your own work, either with parts cut out or, if small enough, as a whole image. Bear in mind that most images on these cards will have a copyright so only use them for your own personal use.

Equally, you can re-use old wrapping paper as background paper, or cut out the images to use as embellishments.

Handmade paper

This section wouldn't be complete without mentioning the lovely selection of handmade papers which are now available. These include the mulberry paper which comes in a vibrant colour range.

Papers can be employed in a number of ways; they can add interest through pattern, texture or colour, and can be used to complement an otherwise small detail, such as a wire flower.

While some papers can be cut using decorative scissors, rustically torn papers can work really well in other designs. To tear handmade papers easily, moisten the edges of the paper and then rip off the excess. This gives a frayed look.

Techniques

Embossing

The term 'embossing' refers to the raised part of an image. There are two types, wet (for use with rubber stamps) and dry (only the dry method is used in this book, however).

Dry embossing

For this method you need a template, a light source (a window or light-box) and an embossing tool (a pen-like tool with a metal ball, which comes in various sizes, see below). Place your template on the light source and secure with removable tape.

Before positioning the card over the template, decide whether your image will be in a raised or depressed form. Both look good, but they are not suitable for every type of card. Also make sure that the card opens the right way according to your decision.

Place your card over the template and use removable tape to keep it in place, ensuring that you can see the image through your card.

Follow the outline of the template with the embossing tool, applying light pressure.

Shaping wire

Shaped wire details can be tricky to master, but the results are worth the effort.

Troubleshooting

In a raised design, slip-ups with your tool can be corrected by expanding the embossed area. A depressed motif can only be rescued with a carefully placed peel-off sticker or a new card.

Use fine jewellery wire and a pair of round-nose pliers for wire shaping – 26-gauge wire is about right; neither too thin, nor too thick. The higher the number, the thinner the wire.

Wrap the wire around a piece of card, then tighten and twist the wire into appropriate shapes for your projects with the pliers. The wire creations on pages 10, 11, 12 and 13 are used in projects later in the book.

Metal thread wrapping

For this effect you need to use pinking scissors, stiff card and metallic thread. Cut a small square from your card with a pair of pinking scissors. Make sure all sides have the same odd numbers of 'valleys'.

Start by fastening the thread in place with a piece of sticky tape on the back of the card. Bring the thread over to the front of the card through the centre of a valley. Go straight across to an opposite valley, over the back, returning to the front again in the centre of the valley next to the starting point.

Continue winding the wire around the card, either in straight, horizontal and vertical lines, or cross over the diagonal lines at the centre of the card for a completely different look.

Once you've mastered the technique, try out differently edged scissors. Whichever scissors you use, the technique remains the same.

Shaping paper

For raised, three-dimensional images it is best to shape your paper first to achieve more life-like compositions. You can achieve this by curving your paper over the blades of a closed pair of scissors. The resulting curl will depend on the amount of pressure you use.

Toubleshooting

Curl the paper in the opposite direction to straighten it again.

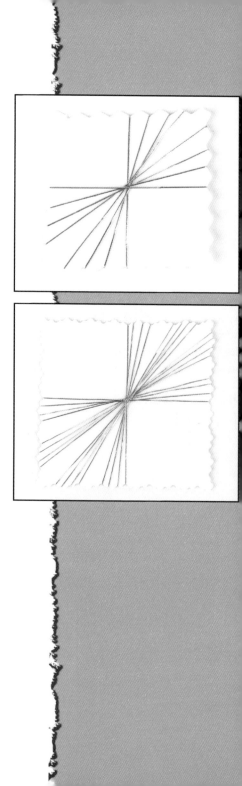

Wire Dragonfly

For a dragonfly, begin by winding some wire four times around a piece of card leaving one end distinctly longer than the other (1).

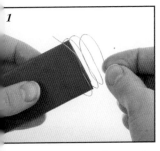

Remove the card, then twist the loops in the middle and wrap the shorter end of wire over the twist (2).

Open out five of the loops and twist any remaining loops together to begin forming the body of the dragonfly. Cut the opposite loop in half to form the antennae (3).

Wrap the loose end of wire around the dragonfly's body (4), and finally give the antenna a small curl. Your dragonfly is now ready for its first flight!

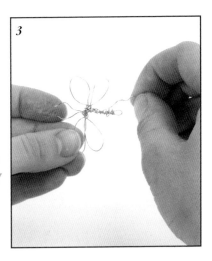

Heart Frame

To create a frame with heart shapes at each corner, begin with a 30 cm length of wire. Shape the first heart by bending the wire piece in the middle. Use the pliers to make a tiny loop, form the heart shape around it and twist the bottom of the heart, so you have equal lengths of wire on either side of your first heart (1).

Repeat this twist and loop process half-way along the two sections of straight wire, making the second and third hearts (2).

To create the final heart, twist the wire ends at the bottom first to form the complete frame, and then shape the heart with an inter-linked tiny loop in the centre. Twist the ends and cut off the excess (2).

This technique can take a little time to master but if you do struggle, slightly easier hearts can be formed without the tiny loop (3). Practise to find your preferred method.

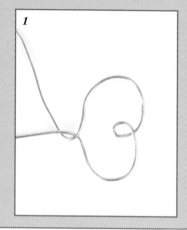

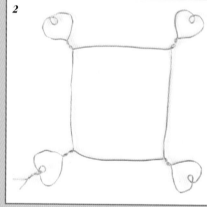

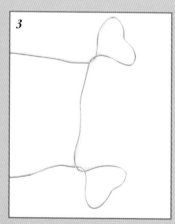

Wire Flower

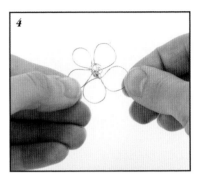

For a flower, cut a small piece of strong card, 5.5 cm wide and whatever length is comfortable to hold in your hand.

Wind your wire three times around the card, leaving the beginning and end of the wire sticking out from the edges (1).

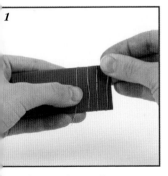

Pull the card out, then punch the loops together and give them a twist in the centre. Wind one of the ends over the middle section to secure the twist (2).

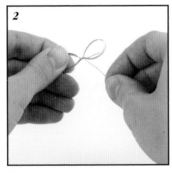

Open the loops and move them into petal-like positions (3).

Curl the loose wire ends over the centre and your flower is finished (4). You can change the petal shapes according to your design (5). Wrapping more loops around the piece of card will create more petals – great for a daisy themed card.

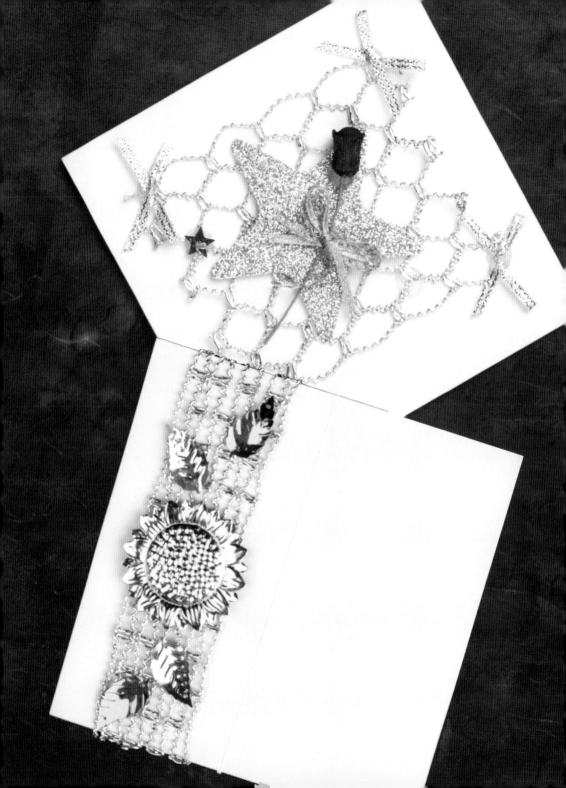

Bringing You Flowers

EQUIPMENT NEEDED

✳ White square card, folded to 12.5 x 12.5 cm

✳ Silver wired ribbon

✳ Sticky tape

✳ Silver metallic pen or strip of silver peel-off sticker

✳ Sticky foam pads

✳ Silicone glue

✳ Metal sunflower

✳ Leaf sequins in gold and silver

Step 1

Measure the height of your card and cut the wired ribbon 3 cm longer than this measurement. Position the ribbon 1.5 cm away from the right-hand edge of the card and fold 1.5 cm of ribbon over the top and bottom, taping in place on the inside of the card.

1

Step 2

Stick the peel-off strip in place, 1.5 cm from the left-hand edge of the ribbon. If you don't have a peel-off strip, carefully draw a straight line with a metallic pen in the same position.

Step 3

Use a sticky foam pad from the kit and a blob of silicone glue, for extra strength, in the centre of the metal sunflower head and stick it in the middle of the ribbon.

Step 4

Glue a gold and silver sequin leaf above and below the sunflower head. Allow to dry and finish off with the greeting of your choice on the left of the card. This card would make a great invitation or 'best wishes' card.

Bringing You Stars

EQUIPMENT NEEDED

* White square card
* Silver wired ribbon
* Silicone glue
* Fine silver thread and needle
* Small star stickers
* Scrap card to make a star shape
* Double-sided sticky-back plastic
* Silver glitter
* Wax paper, or similar
* Ribbon rose
* 3 mm gold ribbon
* Four small silver bows
* Small sequin stars

Step 1

Stretch a piece of the silver wired ribbon from your kit so it opens into a square. Use silicone glue blobs to stick the ribbon to the card and, for extra security, pierce two holes at all four corners of the ribbon and tie or stitch the ribbon down with fine thread on the inside of the card (you can cover these small knots with star stickers).

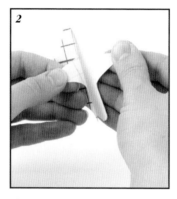

Step 2

Using the template opposite as a guide, draw the star shape onto card before covering with double-sided, sticky-back plastic. Cut out the star then peel off the second side of the sticky-back plastic. Sprinkle the silver glitter over the star and use a piece of wax paper to press the glitter into place.

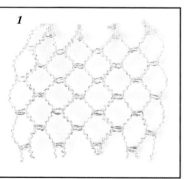

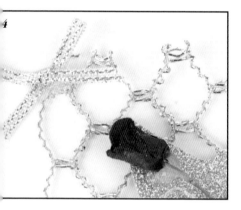

Leave to dry before brushing off the excess, which can be returned to its container. Glue the star at an angle in the centre of the wired ribbon.

Step 3

Glue the ribbon rose across the centre of the star. Tie the gold ribbon in a small bow and use the silicone glue once again to attach it to the rose's stem.

Step 4

Glue the silver bows on all four corners of the stretched ribbon, covering your stitches.

Step 5

Add a greeting to the front of the card, if appropriate, and glue additional sequin stars to the wired ribbon if desired.

Star template

Handy hint

Why not re-use an old gift tag instead of making the large silver star? You'll find it both quicker and a lot less messy!

Bags Full of Greetings

Step 1

Make a start by photocopying the bag template on page 20 and enlarging it to the required size. Transfer the dimensions of your enlarged template to a stiff piece of corrugated card and cut out. Alternatively, you could use old card and cover it with decorative paper. (Glue this paper in place before cutting the bag out.)

Step 2

Fold the bag in half along the marked line. Cut around all the inner lines of the handle, apart from the bottom line which should be carefully scored so you can easily fold the flap down to be opened or closed.

Step 3

Attach a small piece of Velcro™ to the flap and top of the bag to keep it closed.

3

EQUIPMENT NEEDED

For both bags:

* Corrugated card, 11 x 17 cm

* Decorative paper

* Scissors and craft knife

* Velcro™

* Metallic card

* Glue (paper and silicone)

* Raffia

* Ribbon flowers

* Flower sequins

* Peel-off stickers

* White card, 11 x 17 cm

* Velvet flock paper

Step 4

To create a different coloured handle for your bag, use the handle template below and draw it onto metallic card, cut it out and glue into place.

Step 5

Decorating your bag is the fun bit and can be varied to suit the person you are giving it to, or the occasion. This example secures a small raffia bow in place using silicone glue. Small, decorative, ribbon roses are glued on top of flower sequins before being glued onto the bag.

Lastly, gold peel-off stickers are added for extra interest. Your message can then be written directly on the inside of the card, or add a paper insert before writing your greeting.

Bag template

At 50 per cent of actual size

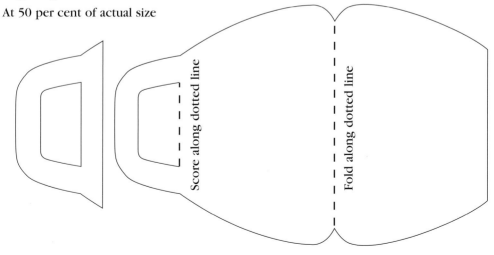

Score along dotted line

Fold along dotted line

Pleated Bag

Step 1

Following the basic steps from the previous project, photocopy and transfer the template for the pleated bag onto stiff card.

Step 2

Glue any decorative paper onto the card before cutting and folding the bag. If you don't have card in the right length, turn the bottom of the template into a single fold or glue an extra piece of card onto the back fold-line.

Step 3

Decorate as you wish to suit the occasion. This bag-card is made from velvet paper, while the handle section and clasp are in copper effect card. As before, gold peel-offs add the finishing touches.

3

Pleated bag template

At 50 per cent of actual size

Fold along dotted lines

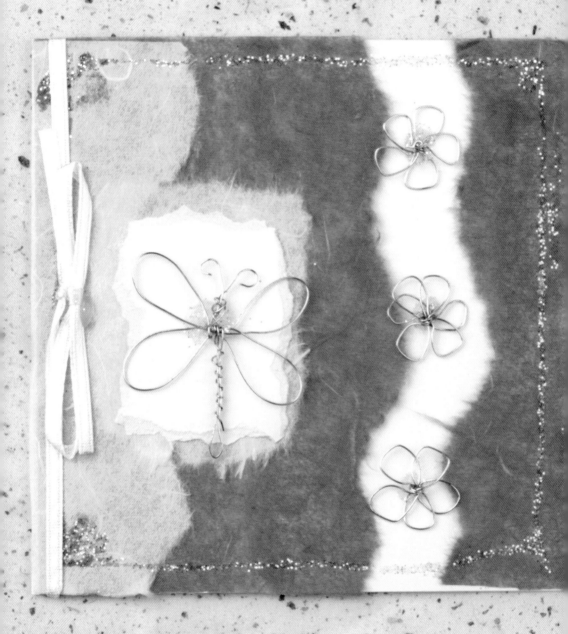

Wired Dragonfly Card

EQUIPMENT NEEDED

* White card, folded to 12.5 x 12.5 cm

* Silver wire

* Blue and mauve mulberry paper, 12.5 x 10.5 cm

* Glue (paper, silicone or glue gun and glue pen)

* White paper or card, 6 cm x 6 cm

* White crystal glitter

* Light blue ribbon, 30 cm

Step 1

Refer back to pages 11 and 13 in the basic techniques section and follow the instructions to make one wire dragonfly and three wire flowers.

Step 2

Take the mauve mulberry paper and tear off a wavy strip from the shorter side approximately 2.5 cm wide, wetting along the tear line first. Glue the two sections of paper to the opposite sides of the card leaving a gap in between as shown.

Step 3

Along the 12.5 cm edge, tear a wavy line (4 cm wide) as in step 2. Glue this on top of the mauve paper along the left-hand edge.

Step 4

Rip a 5.2 x 6.3 cm section from the remaining blue mulberry paper and glue into the position as shown. Tear a small piece of white paper, 4 x 5 cm, and glue on top of the blue paper.

Step 5

After the glued papers have dried use a glue gun, or silicone glue, to stick your wire embellishments into place. Leave to dry.

Step 6

Use a fine-tipped glue pen to draw a border 5 mm in from the edge of your card. Sprinkle glitter over the wet glue and brush off the excess.

Step 7

To finish, use a length of the ribbon and tie a large bow around the front flap of the card near the spine. This project would make a great card for a teenage girl.

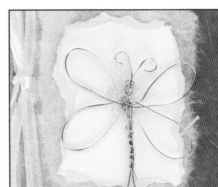

Coffee Time

EQUIPMENT NEEDED

* White card, folded to 12.5 x 12.5 cm
* Pencil and ruler
* Glue (paper and silicone)
* Dark green card, 5 x 12.5 cm
* Lime green card, 1.5 x 12.5 cm
* Brown card, 5.5 cm square
* Hessian fabric, 5.5 cm square
* Silk leaves
* Coffee beans

Step 1

Measure one centimetre in from the spine of the white card and draw a faint guideline. Glue the dark green card along this line, then glue the lime green card directly alongside, as shown.

Step 2

From the middle of the lime green card, mark two points 2 cm from the top and the bottom. Glue the brown square in a diamond position lining up the corners with the pencil marks.

Step 3

Fray the edges of the hessian fabric. Using a stronger glue, such as silicone, glue the hessian square on top of the brown card, as shown.

Step 4

Cut the stems off the silk leaves and glue them into place, overlapping the hessian and brown card in the top right-hand corner. Place smaller blobs of glue underneath the leaves to give them extra shape.

Step 5

Try out several arrangements with the coffee beans before gluing them into their final positions. If you wish, add a greeting to suit the occasion. This card would be ideal for a male relative's birthday.

Handy hint

Why not use other items normally found in the kitchen? Sticks of cinnamon, star anise and dried bay leaves would work really well.

Birthday Fishes

EQUIPMENT NEEDED

* White card, folded to 12.5 x 12.5 cm

* Fish and wave shapes

* Glue (paper and silicone)

* Dark blue paper, 9 x 9 cm

* Mid blue paper, 8.5 x 8.5 cm

* Cream or light sand coloured paper, 8 x 8 cm

* Sack linen, 5.5 x 5.5 cm

* Holographic card, 5 x 5 cm

* Blue gossamer, 4.5 x 4.5 cm

* Pink marabou feather piece

* Eyelets, 1 large, 3 small

Step 1

You'll find similar fish and sea shapes at any good craft shop, but if you can't get hold of them then begin by copying the templates provided onto thick card, colour and cut out.

Step 2

Glue your paper pieces in the centre of the white card starting with the largest dark blue sheet, followed by the mid blue and cream papers.

Step 3

Glue the sack linen 0.5 cm from the top left-hand corner of the cream card. Add the holographic card a step down on top of the sack linen as shown. The blue gossamer fabric is then glued at an angle on top of the holographic card.

Step 4

Stick the fish and the wave in place and add a tiny bit of marabou feather. Use one large and three small silver eyelets to create the bubbles, or you could use silver crystals instead.

Step 5

Add the greeting of your choice – you could use this card for most birthdays but it makes a fun and stylish card for a male relative.

Fish template

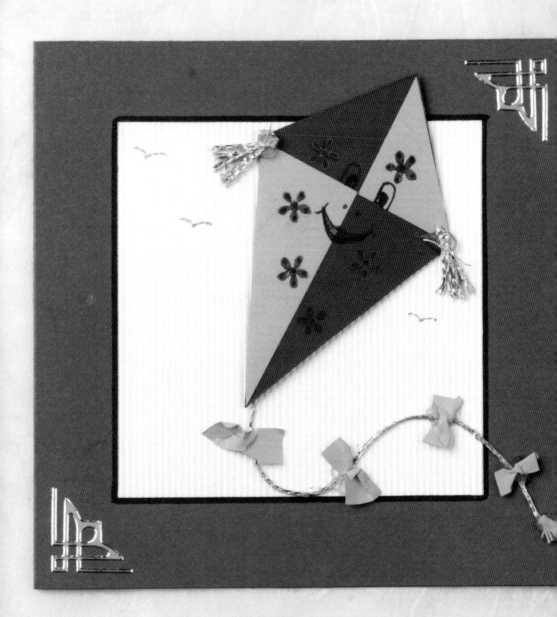

Flying High

EQUIPMENT NEEDED

* Dark blue card, folded to 12.5 x 12.5 cm

* Ribbed white or pearlescent card, 8.5 x 8.5 cm

* Glue (paper and silicone)

* Pen

* Thin red and yellow card, 6 x 10 cm

* Scissors

* Gold string, 15 cm

* Sticky foam pads

* Corner stickers

Step 1

Mount the white card in the centre of the blue card. Use a dark pen colour to draw a frame around the edge and set aside.

Step 2

To make the kite, copy the template onto your red card and cut out. Use the template again to cut and glue two 'quarters' from the yellow paper, as shown. Decorate as you wish, by drawing a face or flowers.

Step 3

Cut a length of the gold string and use silicone glue to stick the cord in a wavy 'windswept' line to create the kite's tail. Cut tiny rectangles of yellow paper and twist them into shape to make the bows, then glue these in place.

Step 4

Position your kite on the white card, ensuring that the kite's tail comes out from under the bottom point. Secure with glue and a sticky foam pad.

Step 5

Make a pair of tassels by tying together short lengths of gold string. Use silicone glue to stick the tassels on the left and right points of the kite. Finish by drawing a few bird silhouettes in the sky and by adding the corner stickers.

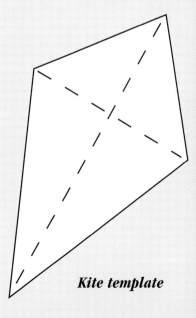

Kite template

Daisy, Daisy

EQUIPMENT NEEDED

* Three daisy punches, 3, 2 and 1 cm in diameter

* Pink card, folded to 12.5 x 12.5 cm

* Pearlescent paper, 12 x 12 cm

* Vellum paper

* Smooth white paper

* Pearlescent paper

* Pink ribbon

* Glue (paper and silicone)

* Fine embossing tool

* Scissors

* Brush pens or pencils

Step 1

Using a large (3 cm) daisy punch, cut four daisies out from the front corners of the pink card. Keep the cut-out daisies for later.

Step 2

Glue the pearlescent 12 cm paper on the inside of the card, so the shiny side shows through the daisy shapes at the front.

Step 3

Using the 3 cm punch again, cut four daisies from the second piece of pearlescent paper. Using a 2 cm medium punch, cut out eight daisies from the vellum paper and a 1 cm punch to cut 16 daisies from the white paper.

Step 4

With your fine embossing tool, score a line lengthways in each of the large daisy petals. Then, by pulling them over the closed edge of a pair of scissors, shape them to create a more flower-like appearance (see page 10).

4

Step 5

Glue the pink daisies over the cut-out daisies on your base card, but at a twisted angle, so you can see the pearlescent paper underneath. Glue the four large pearl daisies in-between the pink ones as shown.

Step 6

Shape the vellum paper daisies over the scissors to give the petals a slight curl and glue on top of all the large daisies.

Step 7

Colour the centres of all sixteen small daisies as shown below: light yellow first, followed by a half moon of orange yellow, finishing with tiny orange dots in one half of the centre.

Step 8

Shape the petals of the small flowers as before and glue them on top of all the large daisies, then glue the remaining eight flowers in a circular pattern as shown in the main picture.

Step 9

Finish by adding the ribbon tied in a bow, or a suitable greeting.

Handy hint

Changing the colour of the base card to a lime green, lilac etc, will change the mood of this greetings card so that it can be used for different people. It's great for a young girl's birthday and by simply placing a favourite animal, toy etc in the centre, you can personalise it even more. If you can't get hold of three punches why not look out for wrapping paper with different sized flowers? Carefully cut the flowers out, curve them in the same way and copy the composition of this card to create a similar effect.

Butterfly Kisses for Mother's Day

Step 1

Use a soft pencil and a ruler to measure and mark a 3 cm border all the way around the front of your card. On the front of the white card, use the metal ruler and embossing tool to press along the lines of the 3 cm square. On the inside of the card, draw a second square 3.5 cm in from the edge, and emboss along the lines as before. Rub out the pencil lines on the outside and inside of the card.

Step 2

On the inside left of the card, use the metal ruler and craft knife to cut a line from the top left-hand corner to the bottom right-hand corner of the smaller embossed square.

Cut a second line connecting the remaining corners. Fold the flaps back along the embossed line made in step 1 so that they protrude at the front of the card.

2

Step 3

Using the corner punch, cut out sections from the folded out triangles. Retain the cut out pieces which will be used later as decoration.

Step 4

Cut a 12 cm square of sky patterned paper and glue to the inside left of the card. If you can't find printed sky paper, improvise, and cut out a section of sky from an old calendar, greeting card or advert.

Step 5

Place your chosen butterfly onto the acetate sheet and cut it out. Carefully cut between the wings and gently curve each one over your scissors to create a more life-like shape. Place a blob of silicone glue under the body and stick the butterfly at an angle in the centre of the sky paper.

Step 6

To finish, add a few bird lines in the sky and stick the punched out pieces from step 3 onto the corners of the card.

Handy hint

Glue an insert in the centre of the card to give it a more elegant finish. Add a hand-written greeting or find a suitable peel-off for the occasion. This project works well as a Mothering Sunday card, but you could use it for a birthday.

Here's to Dad

EQUIPMENT NEEDED

- ❋ Maroon ribbed card, folded to 10.5 x 12.5 cm
- ❋ White gloss card
- ❋ Scissors or craft knife
- ❋ Pencil and paints
- ❋ White 'puff up' paint
- ❋ Dark green card or paper, 6.5 x 6.5 cm
- ❋ Yellow card or paper, 8 x 8 cm
- ❋ Deckle-edged craft scissors
- ❋ Glue (paper and silicone)
- ❋ Light green card or paper, 7 x 7 cm
- ❋ Sticky foam pads
- ❋ Paper gloss or nail varnish
- ❋ String, 10 cm

Step 1

Enlarge and copy the template onto glossy card and cut out. Use a soft pencil to draw circles onto the glass and colour in using pale oranges and yellows.

Step 2

Produce the foam by using a white, heat-rising paint, which is available in different brands (follow the manufacturer's instructions to get the best results), or use a piece of white sponge or felt instead.

Step 3

Cut the edges of the dark green and yellow paper with the deckle-edged scissors. Glue the yellow square straight onto the maroon card, nearer to the top of the card as shown. Glue the light green square slightly twisted onto the yellow square, followed by the dark green paper, which should also be slanted.

Step 4

Use sticky foam pads to glue the glass on top of the layered cards. Apply a layer of paper gloss, or clear nail varnish to the glass, leave to dry and repeat until you get a thick glossy finish.

Step 5

Tie the length of string into a bow and glue in position.

Glass template
At 75 per cent of actual size

Hearts and Roses

EQUIPMENT NEEDED

* ✱ Cream card, folded to 12.5 x 12.5 cm

* ✱ Corrugated white card, 9 x 9 cm

* ✱ Fine mesh red ribbon 4 cm wide, 12 cm long

* ✱ Glue (paper and silicone)

* ✱ Pattern-bladed craft scissors

* ✱ Corrugated cream card, 4 x 4 cm

* ✱ Gold and cream card scraps, or pre-cut heart shapes

* ✱ 4 cm length of 5 mm cream ribbon

* ✱ Pink rose head

* ✱ Gold pen or gold peel-off stickers

Step 1

Position the red ribbon 1 cm in from the right-hand side of the white corrugated card (grooves horizontal). Using some glue, fix it in place on the back of the card.

Handy hint

If you can't get your hands on red ribbon with glitter you can easily add your own with a little bit of glue and coloured glitter.

Step 2

Using a pair of craft scissors, trim the piece of cream corrugated card to give it a decorative edge. Place the card in a diamond position, the top and bottom corners in line with the red ribbon. Glue in place using silicone glue.

Step 3

Glue the gold and cream hearts together, one larger than the other, in the centre of the small square. Fold the thin, cream ribbon over in a loop and glue in the middle of the hearts along with the rose head.

Step 4

Leave the glue to dry then secure the white card in the middle of the cream base card. Draw a line around the white card with a metallic gold pen or use peel-off border lines as a frame.

Handy hint

By changing the colour of the ribbon, you can create different cards. Also, why not use a four-leaf clover for a great 'good luck' card.

Sealed with a Kiss

Step 1

Enlarge and copy the envelope template onto the tracing paper, cut out, fold along the dotted lines and glue the sides together.

Step 2

Decorate the envelope with your choice of peel-offs and stickers. Insert a hand-written greeting or just the heart sequins, as shown. Use a tiny piece of sticky foam to seal the envelope.

Step 3

Glue the corrugated card in the middle of your base card and glue the holographic card on top at an angle.

Step 4

Decorate the card with two parallel peel-off strips near the card's spine and additional heart peel-offs, as shown.

Step 5

Finish by securing the envelope in place with a sticky foam pad.

Handy hint

You could make this card for any occasion, simply change the contents of the envelope. A small note or a poem would make a really personal and touching greeting.

EQUIPMENT NEEDED

* Cream card, folded to 12.5 x 12.5 cm

* Thin tracing paper, 6.5 x 10 cm

* Scissors

* Glue (paper and silicone)

* Peel-off and small rose stickers

* Heart sequins

* Sticky foam pads

* White corrugated card, 7 x 7 cm

* Holographic card, 5 x 5 cm

Envelope template
At 75 per cent of actual size

White Wedding

EQUIPMENT NEEDED

* A4 cream or white card

* Metal ruler and pencil

* Embossing tool

* Craft knife and scissors

* Double-sided tape

* Assorted white background paper

* Gold, silver and white embellishments

* Glue (paper and silicone)

Step 1

Photocopy and enlarge the pyramid template to the required size. Transfer the dimensions of this enlarged template onto your white or cream card and cut out.

Step 2

On the back of your card, use a metal ruler and an embossing tool to score all the dotted lines.

Step 3

Bend all the folding lines to the reverse of the card and fold together to check if everything fits. Stick a narrow piece of double-sided sticky tape on the joining strip, but don't construct the pyramid just yet.

Step 4

Draw and cut out three, 8.5 cm sided triangles from the white background paper. Choose really good quality paper with an interesting finish.

Pyramid template

At 50 per cent actual size

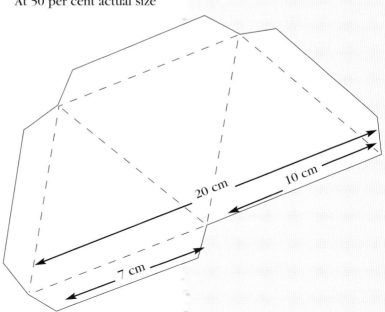

20 cm

10 cm

7 cm

Step 5

Select three different but complementary embellishments. To duplicate the pictured example begin by cutting out three small rectangles from some glitter card, tie three tiny bows out of silver thread and glue them onto the presents. Overlap these presents before sticking them onto the background paper.

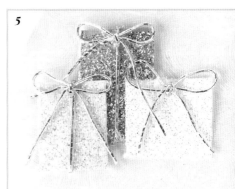

Step 6

For the second triangle, use two plastic rings and glue them together as though intertwined. Gather together a fabric flower, a feather or piece of marabou feather and a bow, assemble the items as shown above then stick onto the paper.

Step 7

For the last triangle, use two small card bells (a bell punch would give the perfect sized bells) and thin gold thread tied in a bow. Secure with silicone glue and leave all three triangles to dry.

Step 8

Once the decorations are secure, glue or tape the triangles onto the base card. The card is now ready to construct or post (see handy hint).

Handy hint

For posting the card, write your message on the back. If you plan to surprise someone then fit the card together and write your message on a separate piece of paper and place it inside the pyramid. The same goes for a small present. Seal the bottom of the pyramid with a triangle of card or paper which can be easily pierced.

Wedding Bouquet

EQUIPMENT NEEDED

* Al fresco patterned mica pearl card folded to 12.5 x 12.5 cm, or similar

* Pearl finish lilac paper, 8 x 8 cm

* Glue (paper and silicone)

* Cathedral pattern-bladed craft scissors

* Cream linen finish card, 8.5 x 8.5 cm

* Filament gold thread

* Embossing tool

* White material heart shape

* Ribbon bouquet in lilac

Step 1

Glue the lilac pearl paper in the centre of the micra pearl card, in a diamond position (see main picture on page 42).

Step 2

Use your cathedral scissors and cut around the square linen card. If you can't find cathedral pattern-bladed scissors then use a scallop pattern or, failing this, pinking scissors.

Step 3

Start winding the gold thread over the linen card. Stick the beginning of the thread on the back of the card piece, come up in the centre of any of the four edges, go straight across the front of the card and over to the back. Bring the thread up one notch left from the starting point. Go across and down on the right side of the first line. Go back under the card and come up in the notch to the left of the previous one and so on for about eight wraps. (See the basic techniques section page 10.)

Step 4

Decorate the remaining two corners with dry embossed lines (see page 9). Glue the thread-wrapped card on top of the lilac paper.

Step 5

Place the white material heart and the lilac bouquet in the middle and secure with silicone glue.

Place Cards

EQUIPMENT NEEDED

* ✱ Two linen finish pieces of card, 10 x 10 cm
* ✱ Pinking scissors
* ✱ Two linen finish pieces of card, 5.5 x 5.5 cm
* ✱ Gold thread
* ✱ Embossing tool
* ✱ Glue (paper and silicone)
* ✱ Scrap of silver card
* ✱ Permanent marker
* ✱ Ribbon bouquet

Step 1

Fold the 10 cm square base card in half. Use the pinking scissors and cut around the edges of the small squares of card.

Step 2

Use the gold thread and repeat the winding process from step 3 on page 45 on both of the cards. Emboss the other corners and glue to the front of the folded card as shown.

Handy hint

To highlight the small card use metallic pens and follow the cut line of the scissors.

Hat template

Step 3

Copy the top hat template onto silver card, cut out and colour the band using the marker pen. Glue the hat in the middle of one of the squares (see page 42). On the second square add the ribbon bouquet. Finish by writing in the names of your guests.

Baby Greetings

EQUIPMENT NEEDED

* A4 cream or white card
* Craft knife and scissors
* Metal ruler and pencil
* Embossing tool
* Double-sided tape
* Pink heart–patterned background paper
* Glue (paper and silicone)
* Border peel-off stickers
* Baby-themed wrapping paper
* White ribbon, 10 cm

Step 1

Photocopy and enlarge the pyramid template from page 43, then copy the shape onto your white or cream card and cut out.

Step 2

Use the metal ruler and embossing tool to score all the dotted lines on the reverse of the card.

Step 3

Bend all the folding lines to the inside of the card and fold together to check everything lines up. Stick a narrow piece of double-sided sticky tape on the joining strip, but don't construct the pyramid yet.

Step 4

Draw and cut out three 8.5 cm sided triangles from the pink background paper and stick onto the three panels.

Step 5

Stick the peel-off borders around the edges of the pink paper.

Step 6

Cut out various items from the baby wrapping paper, arrange in themed compositions and glue into place.

Step 7

Tie the ribbon in a bow and stick at the top of the middle triangle. Your card is now ready to post or construct, see page 44 for instructions.

Baby Boy

Step 1

Glue the mulberry paper in the centre of the white card and frame with peel-off strips or a metallic silver pen.

Step 2

Shape the wire in a square with four little hearts on each corner (see basic techniques page 12 for instructions). Cut the blue ribbon in half, and tie one half around the wire ends leaving the ribbon hanging loose.

Step 3

Glue the frame into position on the mulberry square in the top left-hand corner. Decorate the bottom right-hand corner with the white flower and a bow tied with the second piece of ribbon (see page 51 for the finished card). Add your own special greeting if you want.

EQUIPMENT NEEDED

* White card, folded to 12.5 x 12.5 cm

* Light blue mulberry paper, 6 x 6 cm

* Glue (paper and silicone)

* Silver pen or peel-off stickers in strips

* Silver wire, 30 cm

* Light blue ribbon, 30 cm

* White material flower

2

3

Baby Girl

Step 1

On the inside left of the white card, measure 3.5 cm from the bottom and mark a line in soft pencil. Draw a second line 4 mm above this first one. Mark approximately each centimetre along joining the two lines. These will become your guide lines for threading the ribbon through the card.

Step 2

Cut thin slots at the one centimetre marks. Make sure they are straight and only 2 mm wide.

Step 3

On the front of the card, in soft pencil, draw a half square 6 cm high, 3 cm across, 3.5 cm in from the right-hand side, 4.5 cm from the bottom and 2 cm from the top. (Complete the 6 cm square with a dotted line for use in step 5.) Draw a second, smaller half square 5 mm in from the first. Round the corners and cut along the edges, creating a frame shape, but leaving the frame attached so that it can be folded over. From the front of the card, use an embossing tool to score the card and bend the half frame shape round.

Step 4

Glue the pink printed or un-printed piece of paper on the inside of the card so that it can be seen through the cut out frame.

EQUIPMENT NEEDED

* White card, folded to 12.5 cm x 12.5 cm
* Metal ruler, eraser and pencil
* Craft knife and scissors
* Embossing tool
* Glue (paper, glue pen and silicone)
* Pink patterned paper
* Pink pen
* White crystal glitter
* Wax paper
* Thin light pink ribbon, 35 cm
* Thin white ribbon, 20 cm
* Rosebud flowers

See page 51 for the finished card.

Step 5

Using a pink pen, draw a line around all of the 6 cm square. Follow this line with a glue pen and sprinkle with white crystal glitter, press the glitter down with a piece of wax paper. Use the same method to add the heart in the centre square or add the baby's name, or perhaps a small photo.

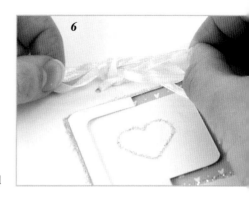

Step 6

In the space above the frame, create two small and centred holes. Cut a 20 cm length of the pink ribbon and thread it, together with the white ribbon, through the holes and tie in a bow.

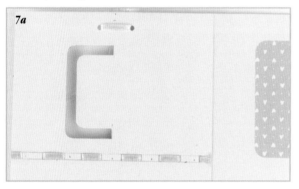

Step 7

Thread the remaining pink ribbon through the slots made in step 2, glue the ribbon at the edge of the card and trim any excess (7a). Glue the three pink ribbon roses along the bottom of the card (7b).

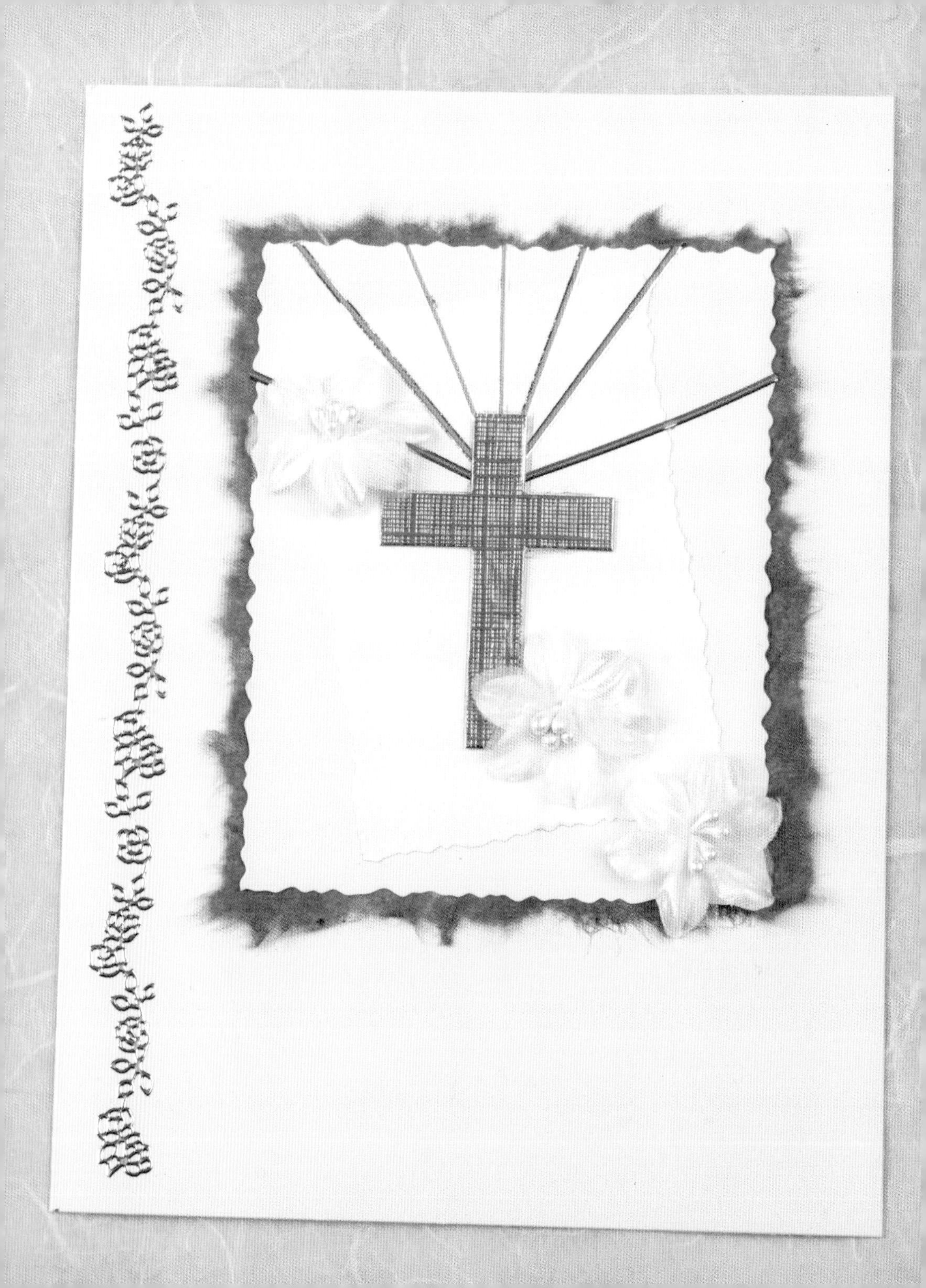

Easter Cross

EQUIPMENT NEEDED

* ✱ Cream card, folded to 12 x 16.5 cm
* ✱ Border peel-off stickers, straight and decorative
* ✱ Purple mulberry paper, 9 x 11 cm
* ✱ Cream card, 8 x 10 cm cut with deckle-edged craft scissors
* ✱ Glue (paper and silicone)
* ✱ White 'hammered' card, 5 x 8 cm cut with a deckle edge
* ✱ Gold cross, bought or made from card
* ✱ Pencil and ruler
* ✱ Craft knife
* ✱ Sticky foam pad
* ✱ Three white silk flower heads

Step 1

Place your chosen border peel-off along the spine of the card, use more than one if necessary.

Step 2

Fray the mulberry paper, keeping it slightly larger than the cream card, and glue into place approximately 2.5 cm from the left edge, 1 cm from the right, 2 cm from the top and 4.5 cm from the bottom of the card.

Step 3

Glue the cream card piece on top of the mulberry paper, followed by the smaller white card positioned at an angle, as shown.

Step 4

Position the cross without gluing and mark the centre point with a pencil. Stick seven peel-off borders radiating from this centre point, out to the edge of the cream card. Trim off any excess.

Step 5

Glue the cross into position over the rays with silicone glue or a sticky foam pad. Stick the white flowers in place as shown and add a greeting if desired.

Handy hint

You could easily replace the cross in this design for another religious symbol, the Star of David would work particularly well. Alternatively, by simplifying the design and using more sombre colours you could use this card to offer your condolences in times of loss and sadness.

5

Crystal Bauble

EQUIPMENT NEEDED

* Cream linen finish card, folded to 7.5 x 21 cm

* Glitter card in white

* Scissors or craft knife

* Thin gold ribbon, 10 cm

* Glue (paper and silicone)

* Scrap of gold paper

* Gold stars

* Large 'hoki' fern punch

* Green and white paper

* Gold string, 15 cm

* Sticky tape

* Sticky foam pad

Step 1

Enlarge and copy the bauble template onto a piece of white glitter card and cut out.

Step 2

Cut two pieces of gold ribbon to stretch across the bauble and glue the ribbon into place (you may need to scrape the glitter off the card in these areas to ensure the ribbon stays in place).

Step 3

Use the template to cut a top for the bauble out of the gold paper. Glue into position. Stick a gold star in the middle of the bauble and two further stars (trimmed to fit) at the edge of the bauble.

Step 4

Punch three fern leaves out of the scrap of paper using the 'hoki' fern punch and, using silicone glue, stick into position on your card. If you can't obtain a hoki punch, then cut similar shapes from green paper, or cut out the leaves from a sheet of seasonal paper.

Step 5

Pierce a hole through the top of the bauble holder and thread the gold string through. Fasten the end

3

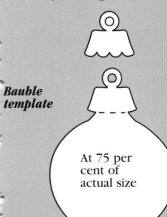

Bauble template

At 75 per cent of actual size

behind the bauble with tape. Use a sticky foam pad and secure the bauble in position on the card.

Step 6

Glue the other end of the string in the middle of the fern leaves, make a double bow and glue this on top of the leaves. Seasonal greetings can be added at the bottom of the card.

Handy hint

If you don't have any white glitter card, spray a piece of card with mounting spray and liberally sprinkle crystal glitter over the top. You could also try coating plain card with glitter nail varnish.

* Green or red A5 card folded in half with an oval aperture

* Scissors or craft knife

* A small star punch

* Silver/crystal gems

* Glue (paper and silicone)

* Thick white paper, 10 x 14.5 cm

* Gold pen

* Selection of peel-off stickers

* Image sheet or seasonal wrapping paper

* Green or red card, 5 x 10 cm

* Gold string

* Sticky foam pads

Festive Fir Bauble

Step 1

Prepare your base card – if needed, cut out the oval aperture; punch the six-star pattern out at the two right-hand corners, and add white dots or silver gems between each of the stars as shown.

Step 2

Glue the paper insert on the inside of the card against the aperture. On the front of the card decorate the rim with a gold peel-off sticker or a pen.

Step 3

Cut out a selection of Christmas greenery from your image sheet.

Step 4

Use the template provided to create the bauble, cut out and decorate to your liking using peel-off stickers.

Step 5

Create a hole at the top of the bauble and thread the gold string through. Hang the bauble from the top of the card slightly off centre and fasten the bauble into place with sticky foam pads. Open the card and glue the loose string ends on the inside. Cover the glue with a star sticker with the ends remaining loose.

Step 6

Finish decorating the front of the card by gluing the cut out leaves into position. Add a string bow and stars to the white of the aperture and finish with the greeting of your choice.

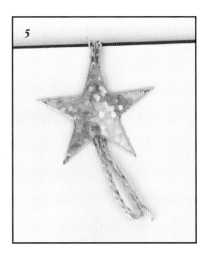

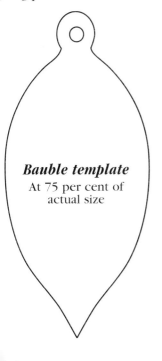

Bauble template
At 75 per cent of actual size

Handy hint

Why not decorate both sides of the bauble and leave it hanging loose? You could also substitute the bauble with an Easter egg, flower or snowflake.

Geometric Christmas

Step 1

Using your craft scissors, cut 5 mm in from the right-hand edge of your gold card, reserve this strip for later. Use double-sided tape to glue the gold card partially under the dark background paper, leaving about a centimetre of the gold card showing on the right-hand side. Glue both card pieces to the base card; 2.2 cm from the sides, 5 cm from the top and cm from the bottom.

Step 2

Use your scissors to cut all the way around the smaller piece of cream card. Make sure the cut pattern lines up with the opposite sides; you'll be using the grooves to wrap your gold thread, which needs to be straight.

Step 3

Wrap the thread over the card going from top to bottom, and left to right. Stick the ends down on the back with single-sided sticky tape. You should now have a chequered pattern as shown.

Step 4

Glue the white card in place; 3.8 cm from the sides, 5 cm from the top and 6.5 cm from the bottom of the base card.

1

EQUIPMENT NEEDED

* A4 cream card folded in half
* Craft scissors cathedral-edged or pinking scissors.
* Gold card, 6 x 11.5 cm
* Sticky tape, double- and single-sided
* Dark green background paper with gold print or similar, 9.5 x 11.5 cm
* Glue (paper and silicone)
* 7.5 x 9.5 cm piece of cream card
* Gold thread
* Christmas tree shape or green card
* Gold pen or dots of peel-off stickers
* Star sequin
* Foil snowflakes

3

Step 5

Use a bought card Christmas tree or make your own using some green card and the template provided. Wrap wire or thread diagonally over the tree and use silicone glue to stick in position. With a metallic pen, or peel-off sticker leftovers, decorate the tree and white card with small dots.

Step 6

Fix the star sequin above the tree and the three snowflakes on the left-hand side of the white card. Place more dots in the middle of all four items.

Step 7

Returning to the gold card reserved in step 1, use your craft scissors to cut two patterned-edged strips, each 7.5 cm long. Glue these strips a few millimetres from the bottom and top of the central white card, as shown.

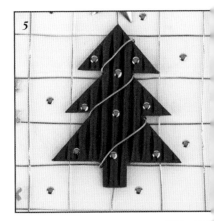

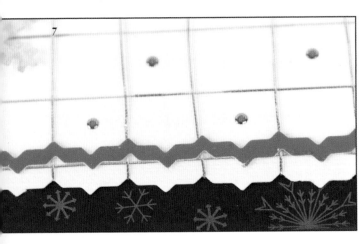

Tree template

Simple Season's Greetings

Step 1

Attach your brass template to a light source, such as a window or light box and dry emboss the top left and bottom right-hand corners of the base card (see page 9 for full instructions).

Step 2

Glue the white glitter and silver cards together, the white glitter card uppermost as shown, and decorate the silver card with the snowflakes.

Step 3

Make a small Christmas tree from the green paper using the template on page 60. Wrap the piece of gold wire diagonally around it.

Step 4

Use a sticky foam pad and glue to stick the tree on the white glitter card; scratch off a little of the glitter to secure the tree more firmly.

Step 5

Decorate with the star and mount the tree ensemble onto the white base card as shown. Finish with the greeting of your choice.

EQUIPMENT NEEDED

✻ Cream or white card folded to 8 x 6.5 cm

✻ Brass corner embossing template

✻ Light box (or bright window)

✻ Embossing tool

✻ Glue (paper and silicone)

✻ White glitter card, 3 x 6 cm

✻ Silver card, 4.3 x 5.5 cm

✻ Snowflake peel-off stickers

✻ Scrap of green paper

✻ Gold wire, 10–15 cm

✻ Sticky foam pad

✻ Small gold star

Ding Dong Merrily on High

Step 1

Take the patterned paper, (you could use good quality wrapping paper), and glue to the front of the base card; the excess centimetre of paper should be wrapped round the spine and glued at the back of the card.

Step 2

Glue the Christmas background paper, which should provide a good contrast to the main patterned paper, in the centre of the card.

Handy hint

If you can't find a wooden bell, you can easily make your own using the template on this page. Simply transfer it to matte, silver card and cut out.

Step 3

Stick border peel-offs around the edge of the Christmas paper.

Step 4

Glue the bell and ribbon into position, as though swinging to the left. Attach the flower sequin at the bottom left-hand corner.

Step 5

Stick the holly onto a piece of paper, cut it out and glue to the bottom right-hand corner of the card using silicone glue, to give it extra shape.

EQUIPMENT NEEDED

✱ White card, folded to 12.5 x 12.5 cm

✱ Green patterned paper 13.5 x 12.5 cm

✱ Glue (paper and silicone)

✱ Christmas background paper, 6.5 cm square

✱ Holographic holly and border peel-off stickers

✱ Wooden bell shape or thick silver card

✱ Miniature bell with ribbon

✱ Flower sequin

Bell template

Last Words

By now you will have discovered for yourself the sense of achievement and fulfilment you can get from making, and giving, your own cards. The projects featured in this book are merely a starting point and your interest in this craft will surely continue to grow.

Take a trip to your local arts and craft shop and you'll soon become aware that there are still plenty of techniques and materials left for you to discover. For instance, rubber stamping and 3D decoupage offer endless design possibilities. Also, look out for new products – the latest exciting embellishments and peel-off stickers can be used to create totally new designs, alternatively, why not return to the ideas in this book and adapt them to suit your own needs and tastes.

Whatever your next project, it's sure to be the first of many – and the only limits to your designs will be your imagination!